For Garrett

An English Room

Derry Moore

with a Foreword by Simon Jenkins

Prestel

Munich · London · New York

© Prestel Verlag, Munich · London · New York, 2013
© for the photographs by Derry Moore, 2013
© for the texts by the individual contributors, 2013
Front cover: Benedict Cumberbatch,
The library, The Garrick Club, London.

Prestel Verlag, Munich
A member of Verlagsgruppe Random House GmbH

Prestel Verlag
Neumarkter Strasse 28
81673 Munich
Tel. +49 (0)89 4136-0
Fax +49 (0)89 4136-2335
www.prestel.de

Prestel Publishing Ltd.
14–17 Wells Street
London W1T 3PD
Tel. +44 (0) 20 7323 5004
Fax +44 (0) 20 7323 0271

Prestel Publishing
900 Broadway, Suite 603
New York, NY 10003
Tel. +1 (212) 995-2720
Fax +1 (212) 995-2733
www.prestel.com

Library of Congress Control Number: 2013938622

British Library Cataloguing-in-Publication Data: a catalogue record for this book is available
from the British Library; Deutsche Nationalbibliothek holds a record of this publication in
the Deutsche Nationalbibliografie; detailed bibliographical data can be found under: http://
dnb.d-nb.de

Prestel books are available worldwide. Please contact your nearest bookseller or one of the
above addresses for information concerning your local distributor.

Editorial direction:
Ali Gitlow

Editorial assistance:
Luna Schmidt

Copyediting and proofreading:
Sarah Kane

Design and layout:
Boston Studio

Art direction:
Grant Boston

Production:
Friederike Schirge

Origination:
Reproline Genceller, Munich

Printing and binding:
TBB, a. s., Banská Bystrica

Printed in Slovakia

Verlagsgruppe Random House FSC® N001967

ISBN 978-3-7913-4729-5

FSC
www.fsc.org
MIX
From responsible
sources
FSC® C022120

Contents

Foreword

Derry Moore is one of today's leading photographers. His career and range of subject matter are exhaustive, as a student of the English face and the English manner but, above all, of the English character. His portraits are masterpieces of human expression, but he is also a virtuoso interpreter of settings, be they of landscape or buildings. He understands the English architectural personality, exterior and interior.

This is a book of interiors, the interiors of buildings but in a sense also the interiors of his subjects as well. It is an ultimate coming together of people and their surroundings, in this case in the peculiar form of a room. It is a book of rooms, chambers, closets, big, small, grand and simple.

Moore's rooms seem to acquire wholly new meaning when peopled by their occupants.

A room without someone in it is always a slightly sad place. The loveliness of these rooms – most of them are exceedingly fine – is enhanced by the presence of humanity. Through Moore's lens the marriage of person and room is always a happy one.

Equally intriguing is how the occupants, many of them well known, take on a new personality when seen in the context of their choices. They acquire a new depth of character as they embrace the enveloping hangings, furniture and objects. Moore is also fortunate that his subjects have expressed so articulately what their room means for them. The picture becomes almost a psychological study.

Few of us probably think twice about our domestic interiors. We know them so well they are second nature to us. But the rooms that appeal to us in other places are more curious. My own affection for libraries is easily explained, in that I love books. But surveying the choices in this book I am fascinated by how others have brought something of themselves to bear on the places that hold particular appeal for them. It is as if the subjects have carried round with them an ideal of a room, a place that does not jangle the nerves or upset contemplation, above all a place of thoughtful repose. It is this ideal that Moore has so masterfully captured.

Simon Jenkins
London, 2013

Preface

Over 25 years ago – which seems like yesterday – I published a book called *The Englishman's Room*. The subjects were selected by my friend Alvilde Lees-Milne and came very much from what might be called 'her world', mainly upper class and all sharing certain criteria of taste. That world has now largely vanished, and when I decided to do a new book along similar lines I realised that it could no longer be more than a pale shadow of the old, unless the basic format were changed. I therefore decided to broaden the selection by including women as well as men, young as well as old. I also extended the concept by inviting people to choose somewhere that held a particular significance for them, a place that could but might not necessarily be their own. I retained part of the original title, and although it could be argued that the title *An English Room* is misleading – we have a farmhouse in Wales, a bookshop in Paris, a villa in Greece, a palace (albeit a ruined one) in India, not to mention plenty of places that are not rooms at all – I feel that there is still an essentially English quality in all of these places.

Some of the choices people made were particularly revealing. Nelufar Hedayat's decision to be photographed in one of the grandest rooms at Chatsworth was quite puzzling until I heard her reasons for this: having just revisited her childhood home in Kabul, which was the embodiment of simplicity, she was taken on a school outing to Chatsworth, which introduced her to a world of unimaginable grandeur and made a profound impression on her. Jeanette Winterson's choice of Shakespeare and Company in Paris was similarly illuminating. This remarkable institution – for it is more than a simple bookshop – had been a refuge for her during a period of deep despondency. The Duchess of Northumberland, who lives in one of England's grandest houses (if one can call it a house), Alnwick Castle, opted for a tree house she had built. This choice initially seemed incomprehensible to me, but once she had explained her rationale it all made perfect sense. It also highlighted a problem faced by those who marry into a grand family and wish to protect their own identity from being overwhelmed by their new environment – an environment in which their spouse is perfectly at home. Sir Humphry Wakefield's great drawing room in Chillingham Castle is remarkable on many counts. This is not simply due to its glamour but because when he bought the castle in the early 1980s the entire place was a ruin – I can vouch for this, having visited it soon afterwards. The castle now looks as if it had been in his family for generations. I found Paul Smith's studio of particular interest. He is a voracious and eclectic collector and the result is a magpie's dream – as well as a child's. There are toys – old and new – shoes and shoe lasts, old biscuit tins and matchboxes, posters, postcards, advertisements, little flags (such as are waved in crowds), articles of clothing – anything that might stimulate his imagination.

Seeing people's choices has been fascinating and instructive. Would my own choice be based on associations or aesthetics, on memories or practicalities? I really don't know. Perhaps it's a sort of eccentricity that appeals to me, a quality that I have encountered time and again while visiting India. There I found the conjunction of the English and the Indian captivating. The result is a form of English – or European – style that has been adapted to the Indian climate, with higher ceilings, deep and lofty porticos, windows frequently surmounted on the outside by eaves that resemble giant eyebrows. Moreover, in the Indian (as opposed to the purely colonial) houses there is a highly eclectic element, a juxtaposition of periods and objects that would make Paul Smith's mouth water. Add to this the light of the tropics filtered through shutters and reflected off shining floors, the whole creating an atmosphere of mystery compounded by the atmosphere of another period. What could be more irresistible?

Tastes change, places change; what is constant is the urge to create a nest, even a refuge. What is interesting is the variety of ways in which people create these nests, sometimes even when the duration of their stay is clearly limited. Even in as unpromising and cheerless a space as his dressing room at the Apollo Theatre, Stephen Fry has attempted to soften the bleakness by introducing some books and a couple of prints as well as a few flowers and even an old soft toy. Reflecting on this atavistic need, I am reminded of a late friend who made a very beautiful library, the object of which, he maintained, was to 'keep the twentieth century at bay'. Perhaps all the places in this book reflect attempts to keep the outside world at bay.

Derry Moore
London, 2013

Acknowledgements

Without the subjects – or victims – who agreed to be photographed and to write about their choices, this book could not have been made and I am most grateful to them all.

Amongst the others to whom I am indebted are Brent Wallace, whose brilliant post-production work was utterly invaluable, as was his patience; and Grant Boston, who is the model of a great art director. Not only does the simple and classic layout of the photographs belie the skill involved, but his help in their selection – always made with great tact – was unerring.

My son, Garrett, has provided both huge encouragement and helpful suggestions throughout the book's gestation, as has my wife, Alexandra. I am most grateful to the Duke of Devonshire for allowing me to photograph Nelufar Hedayat at Chatsworth. Andrew Hansen, my publisher, has shown infinite patience and understanding in the making of this book, as well as insisting that quality should not be sacrificed to timetable. To Caroline Michel, who was my agent, I am grateful for introducing me to Prestel and for convincing them of the validity of the idea of the book.

Gilbert & George

Their home
Fournier Street, London

The furniture in the room is minimal and mostly nineteenth-century. We started to collect nineteenth-century furniture in the mid-1970s because it was both available and affordable. We became fascinated by the period, starting with Augustus Pugin and continuing to Philip Webb and the Arts and Crafts movement. In addition, it seemed to us that it was being discriminated against, just as we ourselves were at the time; anyone who mentioned the word 'Victorian' meant 'Victorian rubbish'. We felt we were in the same boat and therefore felt inclined to defend it. People only collected eighteenth-century furniture, and antique shops wouldn't dream of stocking a piece of post-Georgian nineteenth-century work.

We chose the pieces here carefully. We like to wait until the right piece comes along, like the two small chairs made by Rupert Bevan and two larger ones by George Street as well as a table made by Webb. There is also a George Bullock hat stand, which is similar to the one Napoleon had during his exile. In the built-in china cupboard there are some William Morris Persian vases, a Wedgwood moon flask and a uranium vase made by Bramah. The Afghan rug is not old, but the colours have a soft quality that we like. Between the doors on this (as on every) floor in the house, there is a tiny mezuzah that contains a hand-written prayer in Hebrew – a testimony to the Jewish occupants who once lived in the house.

We like the smell of this room: it comes from the doors which have been painted with pigment mixed with linseed oil and lead, as they would have been originally in this Queen Anne house. The virtue of this mixture is that the colours never fade; the disadvantage is that they take an eternity to dry. We see this room as a sort of common room, free for people to come and read a book in – although there are no books here, we have thousands in our house next door.

We like to look out of the windows into the street to see the reflections in the car windows, roofs and bonnets down below. The reflections in the car windows make it into a sort of *Alice in Wonderland* world.

James Dyson

His office
Dyson HQ, Wiltshire

Large windows overlook the Harrier jump jet perched outside, one of the few not sold to the Americans. It reminds Dyson's engineers what results from ambitious thinking. A brilliant idea – exported to the world. British engineers grabbed the opportunity to turn science fiction into fact, reversing a decade-long trend of aviation disappointment. It is an icon, a testament to daring individuals and perseverance.

Behind my desk is a shelf filled with books about engineers and inventors. Brunel's biography and my Phaidon *Design Classics* are stuffed with my notes and are dog-eared around the edges. In the corner is a round red table scattered with inspiration: models of planes and cars; rapid-prototyped components of our machines; motors, impellers and batteries; my toys. They are always on hand to spark my imagination. I am a tactile person.

When I have an idea I need to sketch it straight away, so my Heron Parigi board takes centre stage. It is the last one in the building. Dyson engineers use computers but I prefer the more traditional approach, armed with my Rotring pencil. It gives a better perspective of how components fit together and a better grasp of scale.

This is not my natural environment though. I am happier in our research and development labs, alongside our engineers. Fortunately, they are just a few purposeful strides away. This is where those ideas become tangible technology, where I prod, query and tweak. When it is ready, it returns under cloak. Blinds down and door shut … it is at last unveiled to the rest of the team; the final step for an idea before it takes on the world.

Willie Landels

His studio
South London

I live in a small Georgian terraced house in an unfashionable street in South London. The house has three floors. This room at the top is my studio where I work almost every day. As I am painting again after a two-year gap, I had to clear the studio of things that came and never left. We also removed 30 cases of books and some of the furniture. I kept art and reference books only. Nevertheless, the tools of my profession take up space. Paint and canvasses have to be kept properly. I used to produce large-format pictures but have now decided to paint on a smaller scale. Restrictions are often a challenge and I think they stimulate the creative process.

The room is white and in need of redecorating. Two wall lights with long articulated arms illuminate every corner. The rug on the floor is a cotton dhurrie. I love to walk barefoot on cotton: as Indians know well, it is a very reassuring sensation. On the shelves I keep many boxes of various sizes. They contain photographs, references, cuttings, prints and proofs of jobs that I am doing, but above all they hide disorder. I cover many of the boxes with paper printed with eighteenth-century patterns. I buy the paper in Milan or Venice: it is called *carta di varese*. Apart from the office chair, I made the rest of the furniture myself.

The room faces east, and on a sunny morning the light is marvellous. It also faces the main road where the traffic can be rather noisy. Fortunately, I am quite deaf and only hear the sirens of the police and ambulance cars. It reminds me of New York in the 1960s.

On the same floor there is my bedroom, separated from the studio by the stairwell that is lit by a skylight. On the landing I keep travel, architecture and cookery books, and also books written by members of my family. I keep them out of politeness. The bedroom has two windows facing west and is very luminous in the afternoon. The white geraniums I keep here are permanently in flower. There is also a small loo with a good basin where I clean brushes and palettes. No doors, it is all open plan. To me, the sense of space is essential.

Tim Knox

The Sepulchral Chamber
Sir John Soane's Museum, London

I am standing in the Museum Corridor at the back of Sir John Soane's Museum. Every part of the museum has its special name, all recorded in the description or guidebook that our founder prepared, which ran into three editions before his death in 1837. The Museum Corridor serves as a sort of anteroom to the Picture Room, where the famous hinged panels or 'moveable planes' are, thickly hung with Hogarths, Canalettos and other treasures. All about us are plaster casts of ancient architectural details and sculpture, ranging from a colossal capital and cornice section from the Temple of Castor and Pollux in the Roman Forum, to casts of ornamental panels from the side of a chariot. But there are also genuine Greco-Roman marbles here, strange columns and feet mostly, and an Egyptian-style lotus capital that once belonged to Robert and James Adam. The dead child is a model for the monument to little Penelope Boothby by Sir Francis Chantrey, the sight of which moved Queen Charlotte to tears. Above, the skylight is glazed with yellow glass, conferring a golden 'lumière mystérieuse' upon the pallid plasters below.

People wonder why Soane, a very rich man, contented himself with plaster casts when everything could have been genuine. In fact, in the days before photography and when foreign travel was difficult and prohibitively expensive, casts like these were the best way of conveying the scale and magnificence of the ancient world to students. Soane was Professor of Architecture at the Royal Academy Schools, and his pupils were encouraged to make use of his collections here in Lincoln's Inn Fields before and after his lectures. He also employed a series of assistants, or 'articled clerks', who laboured in the strange mezzanine that hovers above the adjacent Colonnade – within easy reach of this extraordinary reference collection of classical motifs.

Not everything is classical though. Two large casts are the only surviving record of a pair of medieval carved brackets bearing the badge of Richard II from the Old Palace of Westminster; the originals were destroyed in the fire of 1834. When I came to the Soane eight years ago, this part of the museum was cordoned off and in danger of collapse. We carefully took down most of the casts and the panelling, repaired the brickwork (which was in an incredibly poor state: Soane, the bricklayer's son, had been 'done' by a jerry builder!), installed a steel frame, and put everything back just as it had been. We also took the opportunity to reinstate the curious iron grilles on the floor, which allow light – not too much – to filter down mysteriously into the Crypt below, kept deliberately gloomy, with its Monk's Parlour, Sepulchral Chamber and Egyptian Sarcophagus, and other memorials to the dead. I love this place, and am proud to have played a small part in putting it all back, just as Sir John had it.

Felicity Kendal

The Gielgud Theatre London

This theatre has always been very lucky for me. As well as holding so many happy memories, it's also where I had my first two West End hits. I was first on this stage as a green young actress in 1971 opposite Alan Badel who played Kean in the show of that name. Alan belonged to the tradition of nineteenth-century actors whose personalities were as large and eccentric as some of the parts they played. I was cast opposite him as Anne Danby, a young woman who is in love with Kean.

Alan could act being in love better than anyone I know, next to Paul Scofield. It was, I think, in the way they looked at their beloveds: totally convincing and, like playing drunk, much harder than it seems. He was also brilliant at acting drunk! And he had to act very drunk indeed in act three, but with no time at all between, going through a door sober and coming back on stage drunk. It was miraculous to watch.

Michael Gambon was the joker of the company; he could play a trick on you, make you laugh and lose the plot, while he sailed right on as cool as a cucumber. One night at the beginning of act one in *Round and Round the Garden*, Michael, playing Tom the vet, was on stage. I came on playing Anne and my first line was, 'Tom, what time is it?' – a very important line, as the time is vital to the plot. I looked across the stage at Michael who seemed a bit sheepish. He then glanced at his wrist, where there was no watch, before very, very, very slowly going through all his pockets, twice! He then looked me in the eye and said, 'I'll go and see what time it is by the village clock', leaving me alone on stage! It's best to draw a curtain over what happened next.

Having played a variety of parts in *Alarms and Excursions* in 1998, I then acted opposite Simon Russell Beale in *Humble Boy* in 2002. Simon and I shared communicating dressing rooms and we used to leave the doors open most of the time. We had a jokey challenge game, to see which of us would get the most famous and/or infamous guests backstage after the show. We were pottering along nicely, neck and neck, when one night Simon had A. A. Gill *and* Madonna! With that, he blasted into the lead, until a few weeks later I notched up a couple of HRHs and was back in the game. I can't remember who won in the end; probably Simon.

For some reason, over the years, this theatre has been a charmed one for me and I hold it dear. Moving into the dressing rooms before a run is like coming home, and the stage is a perfect space to work on. It's a beautiful, classical theatre I am proud to say that I have worked in many times with great joy.

Tino Zervudachi

His home
Hydra, Greece

Why Hydra? This new house in which I am so lucky to be able to begin to spend time has been long in coming, but, ever since I first came to the island some 27 years ago, I knew that here was a place where I felt good. Very good. Quite apart from its architectural and topographical beauty, there is something in its simplicity that is both elegant and sophisticated, which I love. It is the crystal clear blue waters, the sky of pale transparent blue – a blue quite distinct from that on the Ionian side of the Balkan peninsula – as well as the balmy (and sometimes very, very hot) climate, the fact that there is no other transport on the island other than one's own two feet (except for donkeys and mules). And then of course there are the interesting people that the island attracts, who tend to become extremely loyal to it… all these things make it unique and not quite like any other place that I know.

The process of acquiring the house, and then fixing it up, was progressive and happened in the most natural way… it was easy and pleasurable, and I hope that this is reflected in the result.

Even though there are a lot of things that were acquired especially for the house, many objects and some pieces of furniture are 'old friends' that have come from other homes or from family. I wanted the peace of this island to be reflected in how the house feels to me. So it is cosy and yet it feels 'light', which is to say that it's not a burden. The house is a refuge to me of sorts, and the sounds that emerge from the small town below such as church bells chiming, cocks crowing, dogs barking or donkeys braying lull me into a comfortable feeling of connection to the place, giving me a real sense of escape from my working life and thereby a true sense of well-being.

I wanted the house to seem as if it belonged here and nowhere else, so the way it is organised – in a relatively traditional way with the kitchen unconnected to the main living areas but to the garden – was planned to make life easier. The accumulation of its contents, which may look as haphazard as it was, adds to the 'story' which the house tells, and which is now part of my own. I feel very much that we belong to each other.

Tino Zervudachi

Monty Don

His farm
Wales

This room is plain to the point of spartan. I like that. It is a curio, different from the rest of the house because the ceiling is much higher and it has a bulging chimney breast but no trace of a fireplace. It was built, with the back kitchen below it, as an annexe to the main house in the eighteenth century and does not quite fit. The two bits of house nudge up against each other awkwardly.

It has almost no decoration, save light. That seems to be enough. The lime-plastered walls have enough contour and shape to catch and spread the light as it crosses the window. There are a hundred kinds of very subtle beauty played like a film throughout the day.

I have had to learn this house from the outside in. When we first came here it was fragile, like a shipwreck, barely repelling the weather and precarious. Over seven years it has been carefully unpicked and reassembled exactly as it was, stone by stone, tile by tile.

In that time the first heart-stopping love has become an obsession. There is a desire for intimacy down to each blade of grass, every tree, every stone in the walls and streams. Every detail has a story that is particular to that place. This series of a thousand details is set against the huge backdrop of the Black Mountains and the present set against the whole roll of history back

to the Mesolithic. I am aware of slipping from time to time as I move from field to field, down the deeply worn tracks to the woods and on up above the tree line onto the mountain ridge. And that sense of history and time flowing through and around me makes the present doubly real and alive. It is a present as free from desire as I have known.

I certainly work hard here all the time. All our heat for cooking, water and warmth is provided by wood from coppiced trees I cut and bring down from the hillside and then saw into logs. I have planted thousands more. There is the feeding of the sheep in blizzards and storms, the gathering of hay, acres of bracken to cut, let alone the constant gentle tending and clearing of waterfalls, streams and paths, trying to become the flow that will take me into everywhere. Everything is hard, everything always steeply up or slithering down, everything demanding real physical effort. Then the house comforts and heals and readies me for the next foray.

I have no real desire to be anywhere else. I ask nothing more from it than what it readily gives. I hope I have enough days left to do half the things I want to do here.

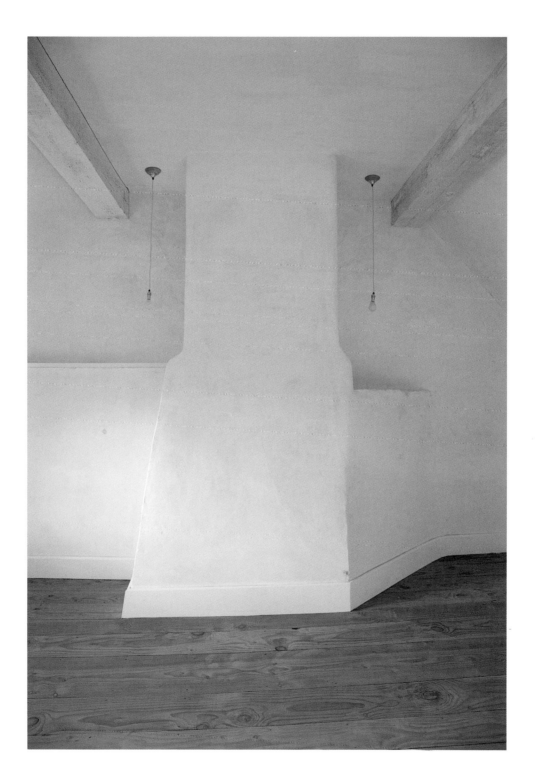

Adam Nicolson

Vita's bedroom, South Cottage Sissinghurst Castle, Kent

I don't usually succumb to the idea of ghosts, but of all the rooms at Sissinghurst, none seems more haunted than Vita's bedroom in the South Cottage. I have known it for 50 years but have never slept in it, or wanted to. It is too dense, somehow, with its own atmosphere. Many other people have occasionally said that they have been mysteriously troubled by something or other: doors closing downstairs, footsteps and, for one friend of mine, a kind of co-presence in the bed beside her. Sarah, my wife, has often remarked that even in the daytime, with the sun coming in through the window that looks down on to the Cottage Garden below, the air feels thick.

It is certainly the one room that connects most powerfully with Sissinghurst's great days as an Elizabethan prodigy house, designed to accommodate Queen and court for their progress through Kent, Surrey and Sussex in the summer of 1573. They came for three days, they hunted in the park, Burleigh and Leicester and all the ladies of the Household among them. They must have dined and danced downstairs.

That, in part anyway, is the atmosphere that remains in this room. Almost all of this great Elizabethan palace burned down in a fire sometime in the late 1760s, but this one corner of the main courtyard, the *cour d'honneur*, survived as a cottage which was then occupied by farm labourers until my grandmother Vita Sackville-West bought it in 1930.

She found this room decorated with several layers of Victorian wallpaper, had it removed and discovered underneath the only complete Elizabethan fireplace to have survived at Sissinghurst. On all sides were the unadorned side-of-salmon-pink bricks of the palace, made more beautiful by the bed of white mortar in which they are set. The walls would surely have been plastered in the sixteenth century, but their nakedness is what Vita loved. When she found the builders, who were making improvements downstairs, applying plaster to her bedroom walls – perhaps according to my grandfather Harold Nicolson's rather cosier idea of what was comfortable to live with – she had them strip it off again.

For the last 80 years, the room has retained the bony distinction Vita required of it. A blue-green tapestry hangs above an Italian bed that, bogusly or not, is carved with the Medici arms and little clumsy putti. The bed itself is covered in a beautiful, browning seventeenth-century counterpane of embroidered plants and flowers. The paint on ancient cupboards flakes and chips. None of the paintings is of any significance. The tall-backed chairs were commissioned by Vita's mother at Knole House in the 1890s as copies of Jacobean originals.

Perhaps this layering is the source of that potent atmosphere: an early twentieth-century idea of an Elizabethan pleasure palace decorated with a faultless sense of fraying grandeur and governed by a wonderful Arts and Crafts tactility in every choice. Maybe it is not Vita's ghost that is here, but the ghosts Vita wanted to summon.

Simon Jenkins

The library
Ham House, London

When I first glimpsed the library at Ham House, it was through a crack in the half-open door when the room was not supposed to be accessible. Everything about it seemed forbidden. The room itself was very small. An old table stood in the middle, piled with leather-bound volumes. An ancient library stepladder was pushed up against the shelves. Two dusty globes and a bookstand were near by. Open on the stand was some ancient geographical tome, yellow with age. Here, I imagined, learningv could be achieved by sheer osmosis. Just sitting in this room would make me wise.

The library, or at least the room itself, was the creation of the Duke of Lauderdale, Restoration courtier and minister, the 'L' at the end of Charles II's hated 'cabal'. He was married to the formidable Elizabeth Dysart, whose beauty and scheming were so much a part of the mid-seventeenth-century scene. Daughter of Charles I's whipping boy, William Murray, from whom she inherited Ham, she reputedly (but implausibly) became Cromwell's mistress to save her husband's life. Lauderdale himself was reportedly of 'ill appearance, his hair red, his tongue too big for his mouth and his whole manner rough and boisterous'. Yet he was learned in Latin, Greek and Hebrew and, 'besides an extraordinary memory, was furnished with a copious but very unpolished way of expression'. He was a true Restoration character.

Lauderdale amassed a remarkable library, but this was sold after his death in 1682. The fittings were moved from the Duchess's antechamber to their present tiny location. The lost books were soon replaced by succeeding Dysarts, and the room was described by an Edwardian bibliophile, William Fletcher, as 'perhaps the smallest of the libraries in Europe, and yet in proportion to its size it contains books of greater value than no other'. Fletcher remarked that, 'There is not a modern book to be seen, nothing breaks the harmony, all speak of a by-gone age'. The collection included twelve Caxton Bibles.

This collection too was sold, during the dark age of country house disposals in the 1930s, and the library stood empty when Ham came to the National Trust in 1948. The present collection arrived at Ham in the 1990s as a bequest from a meticulous twentieth-century collector, Norman Norris, gathered in his garden shed in Brighton. The books, which constitute the finest collection of acquired books belonging to the trust, had previously been acquired by Norris from country house sales, antique shops and auctions.

To sit and occasionally take down and read these volumes is one of the great delights of my time at the National Trust. Ham's tall elm trees, which used to wave in the wind outside the window with their raucous rookeries, have sadly vanished. But the books over which they stood guard are safe. If a library constitutes the soul of a great house, Ham's soul is with it still.

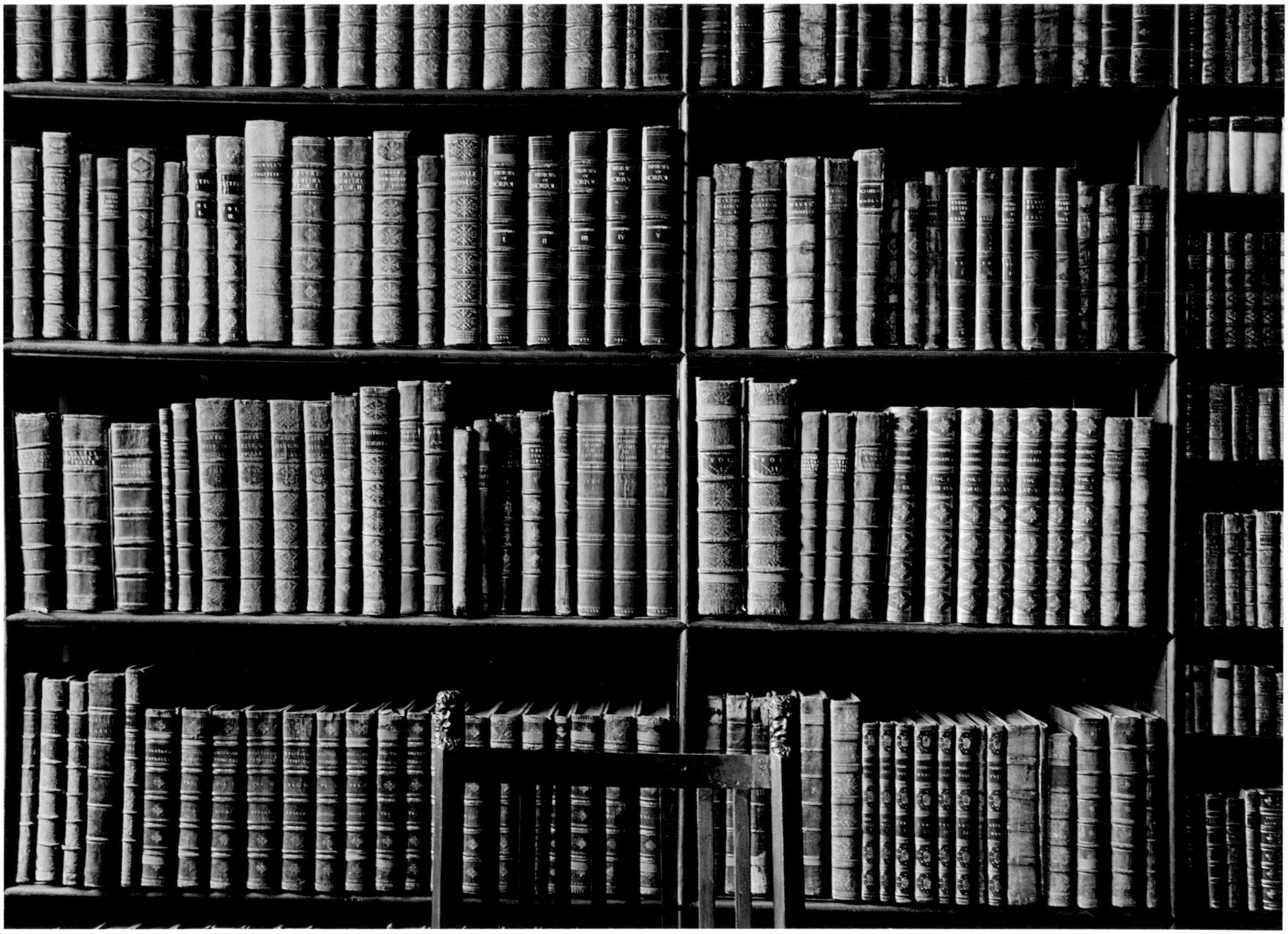

Jeanette Winterson

Shakespeare and Company
Paris

The Greeks had a word for it: *temenos* – a piece of land or a space with a sacred role. Sometimes it was a place of worship, sometimes a place whose everyday function was not its only, or primary purpose. Its reality was part of the invisible unquantifiable world that we know so well when we are in it, and feel baffled by from the outside.

Shakespeare and Company is a *temenos*.

I go there for books. Have you read Lydia Davis's translation of *Madame Bovary*? I go there for company – the best dog and the beautiful owner (of dog and bookshop).

When I began going there George Whitman was still alive. Old as a unicorn, he took over the spirit though not the site from Sylvia Beach who opened the first Shakespeare and Company in Paris in 1919. George's version dates from the 1950s. His daughter Sylvia (named after), still a young woman, is making her own version that began in 2012.

Life is a cover version, and all these versions of the spirit of the bookshop are versions of life itself: various, serious, playful, too much, too little and, more than anything else, an intervention in time. Time that seems to be run for profit by technicians also exists in better versions. There are places, people – even yourself sometimes – that are not in a state of emergency. Finding these better versions of time, place or self seems to me to be important. And a relief.

I love arriving here by Métro. The dog senses me and runs to bury her head in my body. Then there's a cup of tea, greetings, gossip, biscuits, a cast-iron radiator to prop my feet on. A box of books to sit on. No hurry at last. Books and time go well together; the one makes way for the other.

I would be happy to get older and older coming here. When my skin has the look of leaves that have lain too long in the sun. When I am less certain, upright, ready, then the books will still be here. I can lean on them.

I come here in my mind. I bring the rest of me when I can. The odd thing about life is that it is so short. The only way to lengthen it is to live for what you love – and never give way to indifference.

David Mlinaric

St Peter's Church
Hornblotton, Somerset

A few fields away from the Roman Fosse Way, which crosses this part of Somerset, are the remains of the village of Hornblotton. There is now only a manor house, some farm buildings, a broken medieval church tower and, next to it, the church of St Peter. Started in 1872, it was finished in 1874 by Sir T. J. Jackson, a disciple of Norman Shaw. The church presents a complete, but little known Arts and Crafts 'aesthetic interior' commissioned from Jackson by the Reverend Godfrey Thring, and paid for by him and his wife Sarah. She died at the age of 101 in 1891 and there is a memorial portrait of her in stained glass in the chancel.

Everything in the interior seems to have been designed by Jackson. It is all of a piece. There is only one eighteenth-century memorial from the previous church nostalgically reset in the vestry wall, hidden from the congregation. All the walls are decorated with *sgraffito*: two coats of plaster, red under white, and the white coat scratched through in representational designs to show the red underneath. There are birds in the branches of trees, blackbirds and a pelican, leaves and sunflowers, apples, pomegranates and grapes. There are texts from the scriptures, panels of the prophets Isaiah and Jeremiah, Moses striking the rock and the brazen serpent.

Over the chancel arch is the Annunciation in familiar form, as in Old Master paintings, the angel to the left holding a lily. The four Evangelists in blue ceramic tiles are set in the alabaster reredos on the altar and, less Christian, Roman figures in the stained-glass windows at the west end. The mosaic and marble floor in front of the altar recalls the Cosmati pavement in a similar position in Westminster Abbey. The pews, pulpit and other woodwork made of oak, walnut and ebony remind one of fittings in billiard rooms and libraries of similar date and style, all of this marooned in an unspoilt Somerset field, with only a single-track lane leading to it.

The interiors of English parish churches of all dates combine visual references to English social history and art history. They are more often than not very beautiful and, in their entirety, unmatched anywhere abroad. St Peter's, Hornblotton is a very unusual example in its completeness and the high quality of its design and craftsmanship. Even if you are a non-believer, it is well worth going to take a look.

Harriet Walter

Her home
London

These stairs join the 'two-up' to the 'two-down' in my cottagey home in London. Actually, the 'two-down' has been opened up to a surprisingly large space with only a flimsy front door separating it from the garden, a little garden path, a picket fence and gate and then the street.

Coming down the stairs, I look through the window over the front door and see the quiet street outside and the neighbours' cottage opposite. I could almost reach out and touch it, it is so near. A car murmurs by every five minutes or so. At night, a few insomniac cats patrol the street or a fox lopes home to its urban lair.

These are the stairs down and out into the world or up to bed and bookshelves and a hot bath. The trees on the wallpaper reach up tall as a forest, all the way to the skylight in the roof.

This home has always been a haven rather than an entertainment spot, though my few parties have been good. I am not particularly hospitable. I don't have a bursting fridge or a pot perpetually bubbling on the hob. Individuals and small huddles are always welcome to call by, but there will always be more hot debate than hot food.

Behind the wallpaper there is housewarming graffiti, the writings of friends. When I first moved in, recently bereaved and facing a new single life, I invited people to 'bless' the house with a written message or a doodle. They are still there if you excavate.

This house was a new blank page from which to start my future. My time in this house rinsed out the sorrow of the recent past and cleansed and decluttered my life. This house bridged the gap and propped me up. These walls absorbed my screams and bounced back our laughter when, after five years' shelter, it became a home for two.

Stephen Bayley

City & Guilds Art School London

I may look incongruous in my new suit, but I feel comfortable in old art schools – and this is one of the oldest. City & Guilds can trace its history to the day in 1854 when a philanthropic vicar started a drawing class for poor children in Kennington's Black Prince Road. The art master he employed, a certain John Sparkes, evolved this class into the Lambeth Art School and later became head of South Kensington Art School, predecessor of the Royal College of Art. Sparkes, a very busy Victorian, also catalogued the paintings in the Dulwich College Picture Gallery.

Britain's unique art school system is a fine example of our national genius for doing odd things very well. Because of what began hereabouts, every town in the country acquired attractive institutes of bohemia where (as a child I fondly imagined) naked women posed in life classes on wet afternoons and painters in smocks smoked French cigarettes and flirted with students. Later, I found this delightful caricature to be more or less true. But art schools gave us much more. Students at City & Guilds had a working relationship with the local Doulton manufactory. It was so impressive to a visiting German bureaucrat, Hermann Muthesius, that he promptly returned home and wrote a report that led to the creation of the great art-and-industry alliance that became the Deutscher Werkbund. Since an architect called Walter Gropius then took note, it is not too much of a stretch to claim that the germ of the celebrated Bauhaus can be found right here in Kennington.

City & Guilds maintains its independence and I visit whenever I can. Cross the threshold and you escape the fallout of the atrocious Tesco hypermarket nearby, whose baleful influence depresses even the liveliest spirits. There are wonderful rooms with artistic light. On the day this photograph was taken, I found no naked women, but I did find an atmosphere of contemplative calm and a lot of industrious, good-natured students painting, printing, carving and being generally arty. And in front of me? A vast empty canvas. This image, this world, is a summary, for me, of life itself.

Jasper Conran

New Wardour Castle
Dorset

When I first walked into this house nearly four years ago, my overwhelming impression was of light. Light came from everywhere, from the top of the rotunda that forms the entrance hall, from windows and open doors, through which the light seemed to trickle from the rooms beyond. It may sound strange, but I had the sensation of being in a Greek temple, a Greek temple of the imagination.

Soon after that first visit I was lucky enough to buy the house, New Wardour Castle. At one time, soon after the Second World War, it had served as a girls' school – one famous for the naughtiness of its pupils. Several of them have visited the house since I have lived here and are surprised they no longer recognise their former school and certainly have no recollection of having studied in a Greek temple. Prior to its incarnation as a school the house had belonged to the Arundell family, for whom it had been designed by James Paine in 1770.

When I bought the house the walls were of a non-descript white, a somewhat grubby white, and I painted them what I would describe as a definite white. I realised that any colours would be superfluous and that the play of light and shadow would create all the drama that was needed. I also found that the flow of spaces from room to room is so successful – a credit to the architect to which I can make no claim beyond perhaps emphasising it – that I don't really regard the rooms as separate entities.

With regard to furnishing the house I have kept objects – pictures, furniture, sculpture – to a minimum, again letting the drama of light and shadow work its magic. On a sunny winter's day, one could be in the Mediterranean.

Jill Ritblat

The pool room
Her home, London

This pool room is a new addition to a Nash house built around 1820 that received a direct hit during the war and was left a shell. My husband bought the ruin in the early 1960s. It is semi-detached and the other half is intact but rather inconvenient by today's standards. He completely rebuilt and reconfigured our side with Lionel Stirgess and Tom Parr of Colefax and Fowler. For 40 years it was the epitome of an English dream and we did nothing to it until slowly the silk faded, the chintz disintegrated and the light switches began to ooze green slime.

As all the children had left home we needed a different sort of house. I looked for months, during which I saw that so many London houses, however small, were going underground and adding basements that considerably increased their size. Most were adding swimming pools. I am a swimmer and had swum in most public pools in my area, always dreaming of having a pool at home. We both decided that our location and other advantages of the house would be impossible to equal so we drew a big breath and decided to rebuild.

Although my husband loves the eighteenth century, I am a modernist and love contemporary life in every way. Fortunately, it did not make sense to do an eighteenth-century pastiche pool, so we asked Ken Shuttleworth, who had built himself an extraordinary contemporary house, to work with us. It took us five years to work on the plans and permissions, and then four years to build. The specifications are extraordinary – 192 piles around the perimeter of the garden and two 430-foot bore holes with heat exchangers that generate our heating and air conditioning. We worked on the staircase for months, sending the architects photos of eighteenth- and nineteenth-century staircases from all over the world including Viennese Jugendstil, on which the bottom of the Corian staircase is based.

We moved back into the house 18 months ago and still live with a builder in the garage while we grapple with all the incredibly complex new systems. However disheartened my husband was by the work, I began to give parties in this room as soon as I could to show him how wonderful it would be. We had no furniture and there was orange tape everywhere, but I think he was encouraged and we now use it more than any other room in the house except for the bedrooms. We swim and exercise in it, and I have entertained about 600 people at various times over the last year, including for the Cultural Olympiad.

Even though it is a basement the room has wonderful natural daylight and, as it is incredibly simple, I installed both a projector and LED lighting around the perimeter so it is enlivened by light and image. My favourite moment is swimming at night with a saturated pink light washing the walls, which makes the water navy blue.

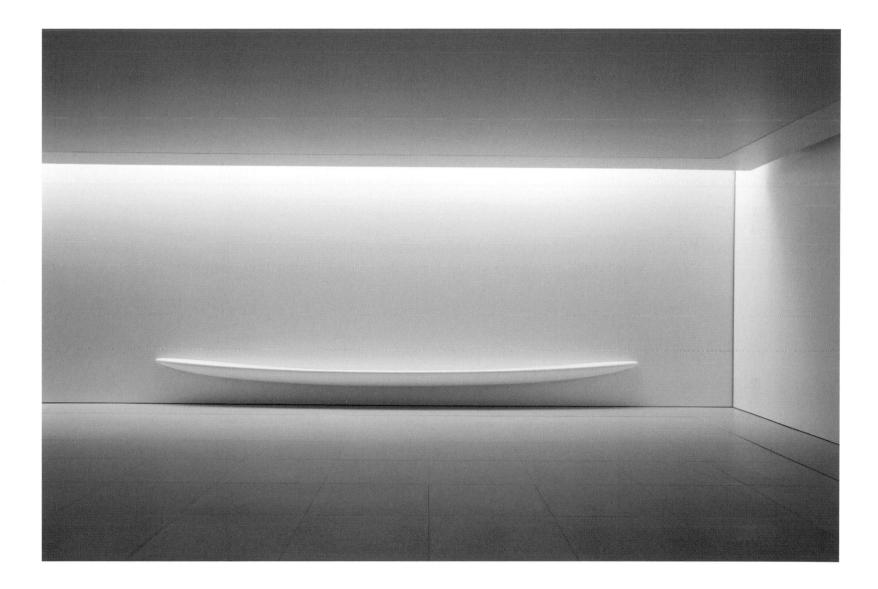

The Duke of Beaufort

The hall
Badminton House, Gloucestershire

I first visited Badminton at the end of the Second World War, when I was about 15. I remember having tea in the housekeeper's sitting room but have no recollection of seeing this room, the hall, on that occasion, which is not as surprising as it sounds since most of the house was shut up and barely lived in at that time. This was because Queen Mary, who had spent most of the war at Badminton, bringing a large retinue with her, had on her departure taken the retinue, including virtually all the servants – there had been about 40 – leaving my poor cousin's wife with a rather decrepit butler to look after her and the entire house. On that occasion, Badminton seemed to me a cold and grim house. I remember that when my cousin, the 10th Duke, who had no children, said, 'I hope you'll make this house your home', I was horrified and thought, 'How awful.'

After that first visit, I frequently used to spend the weekends at Badminton, the main attraction being the hunting. In retrospect, it must have been dreadful for my cousin and his wife when this rather gormless teenager arrived, but they were always kindness itself.

In 1950 I married, and my wife and I would spend most weekends at Badminton. When we bought a house in Badminton village in 1960, I think the Duke was rather disappointed, as he tried to dissuade us from doing so. Not having any children of his own, I think he missed our visits (we had several children by this time), which must have livened up his life. After his death in 1984, we moved into the big house and, although we redecorated most of it, we never touched the hall, which remains much as when it was originally designed by William Kent in the early eighteenth century. This despite its having served as a drawing room at one time, when it was filled with aspidistras and must have been icy cold as there was no central heating. It's the only room in the house entirely designed by Kent, who also designed the furniture. It is a wonderful room, although to my mind not perhaps as wonderful as the Great Hall at Houghton, for which Kent was also responsible.

Alan Bennett

Primrose Hill
London

The room in which I'm standing I decorated myself some 40 years ago. The house was built in 1840, the date and the architect's name scratched on the right of the marble fireplace. I stripped off more than a century's accumulated paint and paper to reveal the original lime plaster. I then painted it with various water-based stains in orange, yellow and terra cotta before finally washing them down and sealing the surface that was left. I hope it looks like the wall of an Italian palazzo. The other half of the room I stained blue, but found this too cold so put yellow over it, which turned it a vivid green.

This process is easiest to do when the walls are of old lime plaster as this takes stain well and shows up the grain of the plaster and anything else that may be on the wall – the builder's notes to himself, for instance, which I left.

Though I no longer live in this house, I've done the same elsewhere and am particularly pleased with a yellow room I've decorated in a similar fashion. With luck, even if papered over, these stained walls will survive me.

Paul Smith

His studio
London

When I was asked to select my most important room, I decided to choose my studio at work, because although I have a lovely room at home full of books, robots, postcards and toys, I spend more time in my studio. It's a room full of lots and lots of things, all of which are sources of inspiration. Anyone who knows me or my work knows one of my popular sayings is, 'You can find inspiration in anything, and if you can't, please look again.'

When I have design meetings around my big table in the middle of the room, I often lean back and pull out a book and say, 'I like the colours in this book'. It might be a book about an artist or old photos, or something very inappropriate like something very old next to something very new, or something very small next to something very big, so it's this constant source of inspiration.

The other thing is I am very privileged to get lots and lots of things sent to me all the time. It's really interesting that people as young as six years old up to people of 90 years of age send things to me and it's not demanding, it's about just wanting to communicate with me – so it's just a room full of lovely things.

Cressida Bell

Her home
London

My kitchen is all about colour and is inspired by the interior decoration of the Grand Bazaar in Istanbul, which mainly consists of royal blue, turquoise, coral and cream. It is incredibly cosy in the winter, yet cool if it is blazing hot outside. Like most kitchens, it is the hub of the house and the place where I am most likely to be found.

I love to entertain, which is a good excuse to collect pottery. My current favourites are the gilded Bavarian tea sets on the top shelf of the dresser. They date from the 1940s and each one has a different highly elaborate design. I also have a number of Turkish plates and bowls and a motley selection of jugs from Spain and Italy. I suppose you might call these things functional souvenirs. They certainly recall different trips abroad and bring me happy memories.

The woman in a niche at the bottom of the stairs was made by my father, Quentin Bell, and I think of her as my 'household goddess'. On and around her is an accumulation of oddities including metal ex-votos, Mardi Gras beads and votive candles which seem to suit her quasi-religious status. I have quite a lot of his work including the pottery lamp (another woman in a niche) and painted shade. On the wall behind is a copy of my poster designed to help people learn to cook by using an easy flowchart. I don't exactly need it, but it goes with the kitchen clock and gives me ideas when I can't think what to make for dinner.

The Marquess of Salisbury

The main staircase
Hatfield House, Hertfordshire

Hatfield was built in a hurry to entertain the King. The man who built it, Robert Cecil, Earl of Salisbury, may have felt more than a stab of irritation at having to do so. His father, Burghley, whom he had succeeded as his monarch's chief minister, had already left him a vast prodigy house a few miles southeast of Hatfield: Theobalds, now vanished. Burghley had often entertained the Queen there, and his son did the same with James I and VI, whose smooth translation to the English throne Robert had arranged with his usual careful skill.

After a number of visits to Theobalds, James began to covet it. He proposed a swap for his empty palace at Hatfield. Even the Lord Treasurer could not refuse such a proposal from his King, but he drove a hard bargain: 19 manors to sweeten the blow. Besides, there was no doubt he would have to replace the fifteenth-century quadrangle with 'a new habitacion'. Theobalds or no Theobalds, the King would still come to stay and Cecil would need a house fit to accommodate him.

This new house was smaller than Theobalds, but matched it in magnificence. It cost about £40,000 to build, just under ten per cent of the revenue of the English crown when Elizabeth died, and was pretty nearly finished by 1611. It left its builder in debt and James never stayed, dining there just once before his servant Robert died agonisingly of cancer in 1612. Robert Cecil's successors have lived here ever since, with a brief break in the mid-eighteenth century when the then incumbent was too broke to be able to afford to occupy the house.

Despite its grandeur, there is something welcoming about Hatfield. Returning after weeks of absence, it receives you with immediate warmth; perhaps because so much of it is panelled in wood and its fireplaces are home to the most delicious log fires that radiate heat across their polished steel fenders emblazoned with unapologetic coats of arms. (Like most parvenus, this family always liked flaunting their newly acquired nobility.) I can think of no other house that possesses so many rooms, grand or less grand, where one would be happy to settle in cosiness and comfort. Luckily, a family still lives here and the cosiness therefore endures. Our visitors notice and approve.

The main stair is not cosy, neither is it comfortable. However, it is perhaps the chief architectural glory of the house. Cantilevered, before such construction was commonplace, its dimensions, ceiling, carved cherubs, beasts, musical instruments and dog gates give it a magnificence that must have gratified its first owner. We have recently restored the ceiling and the walls, removed the pictures and begun to hang tapestries instead. In so doing we strive to improve the patina of the place, while hoping to do no violence to the spirit of the original. Robert Cecil would perhaps have approved of our objective.

Gavin Stamp

The grand staircase
St Pancras Renaissance Hotel
London

The grand staircase in what used to be the Midland Grand Hotel at St Pancras Station is one of the most spectacular interior spaces in London. It goes up and up, rising and dividing, supported on decorative iron beams and enclosed by richly decorated walls below a star-spangled Gothic rib vault. It is a triumph of the great Victorian endeavour to make the Middle Ages modern and a masterpiece of its creator, the architect Sir Gilbert Scott. I first saw it, and walked up it, almost half a century ago and I still find it thrilling. The miracle is that we can still all enjoy it since the whole building was very nearly demolished.

As a schoolboy in South London, I grew to love Victorian architecture and Victorian railways. I was dismayed when I read an article by John Betjeman lamenting that British Rail were planning to replace that wildly romantic and yet practical complex of red-brick, stone, iron and glass, St Pancras Station. In 1966 I joined the Victorian Society to support the campaign against demolition, and on a visit to the station organised by the society heard the architect Roderick Gradidge explaining how easy it would be to introduce modern services and bring Scott's building back into use as a hotel. Thanks to the society and the late Wayland Young, Lord Kennet who, as a government minister, upgraded the listing of St Pancras from III to I, the station survived.

A decade or so later, I gave evidence for the Victorian Society at a public inquiry into British Rail's plan to 'modernise' the booking hall by throwing out the Midland Railway's old timber ticket office. The society argued that this structure could perfectly well be adapted and relocated, and the inspector agreed. British Rail then went into a big long sulk. By that stage I was living in the area and could see the spires and chimneys of St Pancras and the vast bulk of W. H. Barlow's train shed from the upper rear windows of my house – a wonderfully romantic urban skyline. I was therefore able to observe the steady deterioration of the building created by its owner's wilful neglect.

Although the station had never ceased operating (despite sustaining bomb damage in both world wars), the hotel closed in 1935 – an event presided over, so I discovered, by my great-uncle Josiah Stamp, then chairman of London, Midland & Scottish Railway. The building itself limped on, at first as offices – St Pancras Chambers – before being saved by the amazingly imaginative decision to make St Pancras the London terminus for Eurostar services.

Then followed the restoration and conversion of Gilbert Scott's edifice, by now empty and forlorn, both back into a luxury hotel and as apartments. It is all much better an outcome than any of us could have hoped for half a century ago. It is so very gratifying that the Vic Soc have been proved right about the worth and continuing value of St Pancras: a railway station of the nineteenth century made fit for the twenty-first century.

In this photograph, Derry Moore captures me, pensive and alone, on the grand staircase (standing on the splendid new carpet rewoven to the original design), but it is good that others can now enjoy it – along with the bars and restaurants in the carefully restored original rooms. I shall never be able to afford to stay there, of course, but – thanks to the management of what is now the St Pancras Renaissance Hotel – shortly before the hotel reopened in Gilbert Scott's bicentenary year, I was treated to an overnight stay, sleeping in an original Gothic Revival bedroom to test the facilities. It was rather wonderful.

James Reeve

His studio
Somerset

My own studio is only my favourite room because it is mine and I live in it, and shall, until an old person's dayroom becomes the inevitable alternative.

My favourite rooms from the past are by now all dismantled or unrecognisable as they once were, at least as my memory presents them. The lovely ink-blue dining room, for instance, in Bantry House, County Cork, when the eccentric Mrs Shelswell-White was the châtelaine. I once encountered her in Bantry Square, in the pouring rain, blowing her nose on one of the old black-and-white five pound notes she had fished out of her pocket…

Or, in Somerset, Mrs Yandle's larder, with its slate shelves crowded with pans of clotted cream, sundry innards in chipped yellow dishes, bundles of pigs' trotters and bunches of bay leaves, birds as high as kites hanging from butchers' hooks, all overlaid with the smell of pippins and antique stilton and yesterday's fish pie…

Or, my Aunt Carew's Devonshire drawing room, suffused with the smell of wine-red clove pinks; giant Staffordshire figures painted green and mauve and tangerine; the glazed chintz curtains freshly hung for the summer; the gin and French on the refectory table under the school-of-Oudry painting of a goshawk savaging from on high a pair of nesting swans; a length of half-finished gros point abandoned on a sofa…

My room is not only a workroom, with enough paints and turpentine and canvas and stretchers to withstand a siege. It is also a repository, a rook's nest of curiosities brought back from the far-flung places where I have, over the years, lived and worked: Uganda, the Australian outback, Madagascar, Haiti, the Yemen and Mexico (35 years in a jungle and then the centre of the City itself).

I have some thirteenth-century monks' skulls discovered during repairs on a cloister of the Monasterio del Parral, the Hieronymite monastery outside Segovia where I was interned as a novice for a time following my studies at Madrid's Academia de Bellas Artes. The monks had, it seems, been visiting from the brother monastery in Granada, but unluckily succumbed to the plague. So it was deemed by the Prior proper to return them to be buried whence they came. It fell to me – my battered pickup van was still parked outside the entrance gates – to drive the remains, in boxes, to the railway station. En route, the ill-fitting doors were flung open by a pothole and, unbeknownst to me, the road strewn with skulls. In the process of recovery I kept back a few, and have them still: amongst a detritus of stuffed hummingbirds, the feathered capes of African chieftains and their wives' polished teeth set in gold, fragments of Aztec lapis funerary masks, some voodoo dolls from Haiti stuffed with hair…

How strange it is that the room will, as ourselves, be at last disbanded; and yet its parts, unlike ours, will live on in other circumstances and in others' hands.

Nelufar Hedayat

Chatsworth Derbyshire

Time can sometimes be deceptive. I'm the living embodiment of it. In my very short time on this earth, I've experienced how an instant can last for an eternity, as on the occasion when my family and I waited in the passport office in Peshawar to have our British visas stamped, so we could start the journey from Pakistan that would lead us to our new lives in the UK. Days, even months can go by with incredible speed, as in the many happy summers spent playing outside until sundown with all the other children on the London estate where I grew up.

Time and space, for someone like me, born in Kabul and brought up in Camden Town, is a most interesting experience. In 2007, I returned to Afghanistan for the first time since we fled 18 years ago and revisited the clay-and-wood structure in Taymani where I was born. I was overwhelmed. In this small, decrepit room with its dusty floor, threadbare rugs and small wooden table packed full of jars and plates, without history or sense of grandeur, I felt that time had stopped. I felt at home but also abject. Whatever this little clay room was, I knew I was connected to it. This was one of two occasions in my life that a space, a room, would induce such an existential feeling within me.

The second occasion was when I was on a school trip that same year. My tutor at our comprehensive school was keen to get us urban kids to see the British countryside and organised a trip to Chatsworth in Derbyshire. I had by that point lived like many first-generation immigrants to the UK: compromising, negotiating and sometimes contradicting myself.

Visiting Chatsworth was a remarkable experience. The idea that I, born in the third poorest country on Earth, should become a sort of link with what must be one of the most sophisticated palaces in the world, seemed incredible. Every room we entered took my breath away. I thought about the thousands of prominent, talented and privileged people who had walked through them. I marvelled at the Baroque exquisiteness of so many paintings, artefacts and sculptures. I played out scenes of the many dukes and duchesses entertaining the great royals of the land, the whole operation made possible by an army of staff moving around unseen. All of these intoxicating thoughts played out in my head in this grandest of all grand English houses. I felt misplaced and yet entirely captivated by the space. Time once again stood still for me, and I was the last to board the bus back to the Big Smoke.

Edmund de Waal

His studio
London

This is my new studio. The photograph was taken three days after we moved in, so there is a deceptive quality to the emptiness. I think you can feel a breath of hesitancy here, a sort of threshold moment before equipment, the kit of a pottery studio, the books, the archive of works, the bags of clay and glaze materials were unpacked and assigned resting places. This is the pause before vitrines and shelves were put on walls and the first pots arranged. So I look at these images and think about what is to come, the work, the projects, the books that I hope will happen here. And I think of the other white spaces that

I love – the transepts of Lincoln Cathedral, which I knew as a child, the luminous interiors of Saenredam's paintings, the fullness of a Chinese porcelain bowl – and I hope I can keep a measure of this here. I care very deeply about the spaces in which I work and I'm always intrigued by how little you have to do to alter the energy of a room. Many of my installations explore what it is like to put a few objects down in the world and watch what happens. This photograph is special for me. It is my deep breath picture.

P. D. James

Clavell Tower
Isle of Purbeck, Dorset

I first saw the nineteenth-century Clavell Tower in the spring of 1971. It was a blustery day with the tide running strongly, crashing over the black rocks and the friable cliff. I remember circling the tower, touching the time-weathered bricks, recalling having read that Thomas Hardy trudged up the narrow pathway with his first love, Eliza Nicholls, surely one of many couples who have made their tryst at this beloved landmark. There still hung about the decaying tower a vestige of old grandeur and nobility, burdened with the melancholy of inevitable loss. How could it be otherwise? However greatly loved, it could only be a few years before the sea finally won. In imagination I pictured an old man recalling the day when the great storm brought down the last bricks to litter the black shale below. There could surely be no chance of saving it; the work would be complicated, expensive, possibly even a little dangerous, and which organisation would have the money, expertise or confidence to undertake it?

But in 1971 I had not heard of the Landmark Trust, dedicated to saving just such eccentric, well-loved buildings that are so much a part of our English heritage. Rebuilding the tower in its new position must be one of the most difficult tasks the trust has ever undertaken. Each brick had to be individually moved to construct a tower that stands as a tribute both to the past and to the architect and builders, and above all to the courage and faith of the trust.

I last visited the new tower, now standing 85 feet from the cliff edge, on my 92nd birthday – the occasion on which this photograph was taken. It was one of those perfect summer days which we English believe can never be experienced anywhere else in the world. Only the circular remnants of the old foundations mark the spot where it once stood. The new tower is a marvel of elegance and grace, standing as a reborn landmark over land and sea. We sat in the uncluttered circular kitchen, providing everything a modern cook could desire. To walk round the circular balcony above is to rest the eyes on a wide panorama of heart-stirring beauty. No wonder the list of couples anxious to spend a holiday in this newly created and unique building is long.

The old tower, and Purbeck itself, were the inspiration for my sixth novel, *The Black Tower*, where the blackness was symbolic. My visit to the renewed and beautiful tower inspired four happy lines of verse:

> *How sweet the air on field and hill,*
> *How calm this blessed land,*
> *And England will be England still*
> *While Clavell Tower shall stand.*

Sir Humphry Wakefield

King James I Room
Chillingham Castle, Northumberland

Chillingham's King James I Room is one of three royal chambers strung between two medieval towers, built to welcome the Scottish King on his way south to take his English crown. King James came back to these same rooms in 1617 and Charles I came here in 1645 on his way to negotiate with the troublesome Scots.

When I came here in the 1980s this room was a roofless, floorless ruin, its original architecture smothered with rotted Victorian plasterwork. But Elizabethan ceilings and mouldings sprang to life as we recovered the original gilded detail and plasterwork colours similar to those at Knole in Kent.

Chillingham's famous ghosts certainly helped with furnishings. The battered but beautiful Aubusson carpet and the brocaded hangings were both acquired somewhat serendipitously – the vast carpet thanks to a throwaway remark made to the owner of an antiques shop, and the wall coverings and curtains after a technical fault at the Caserta silk mills rendered them unsuitable for their intended home at Chatsworth but a perfect fit for Chillingham!

I bought the room's Irish furniture 50 years ago, when Irish furniture was only valuable if it could be rehashed as American. All my favourite seventeenth-century pieces found their rightful home here, along with a few marvellous replicas of great furniture from my project with the American Baker Furniture Company. The Queen Anne walnut bureau cabinet was one that Peter the Great designed himself for the Hermitage, and the gilded lanterns came from the Palace of Holyroodhouse in Edinburgh. The seventeenth-century looking-glasses, from Italy and England, reflect and inter-reflect to add their own glitter and life.

In the bowed oriel window stands a painted Louis XV bath, carved like a great shell by the ébéniste de la Fosse. This was given to me as a farewell present half a century ago by the furniture dealer Mallett, where I had worked for several years. A marble Bacchus fountain feeds the bath and marble urns and a flamboyant marquetry table, all designed for Versailles, add panache. These pieces were bought during the French Revolution.

We Wakefields are the only family in the world to have the heraldic crest of a bat. So, eighteenth-century bats fill tapestries and porcelain and even border many of the family portraits. These pictures are not of high quality, although the occasional Downman, Herring or Romney raises the tone. Moreover they have a gentleness that softens the room's bright silks and calms the sparkle of the display of weapons and porcelain.

How and why do so many differing nationalities, styles, lacquers, gildings, woods and materials mix so happily? I think the answer is simply because quality alongside quality produces its own synergy, regardless of nation, material or period. This attribute allows me to buy whatever I can afford in my world travels, since the King James I Room will always give it a warm welcome.

Stephen Fry

His dressing room
The Apollo Theatre, London

Were I to be asked if I think of my dressing room simply as an impersonal waiting room – a sort of holding point between my present persona and the stage – the answer would definitely be no.

I'm a huge nester. I'm never satisfied until I've got cards, cutlery, glassware, a well-stocked fridge and so on. I even hammer in hooks so I can hang pictures. During the run of the play my dressing room becomes for me a kind of drawing room in the West End, which is a nice luxury.

I like to arrive early before the performance and I always listen to the sound relay speaker that all dressing rooms have so that I can hear how the play is going when I'm not on stage.

I sympathise with John Gielgud, who remarked that in times of 'great stress, nervousness, despondency, failure or success' his dressing room was a refuge from outside interference. Luckily, most other actors don't visit you in your dressing room unless you specifically arrange it – privacy and being allowed to sink into your own thoughts is important. I would hate it if anyone visited me before the performance, although afterwards I really like it. I keep wine and drinks and enjoy seeing friends – providing, of course, the show has gone well.

Carole Bamford

The tithe barn
Daylesford, Gloucestershire

The tithe barn has always been a favourite building on the estate. Built in the late eighteenth century, its simple cruciform shape seems to be at the heart of everything, so it was an obvious place to make my office and studio. I walk in and feel immediately at peace. I travel a great deal and so, when I come home, it is important to have somewhere I feel immediately grounded and happy, surrounded by favourite things. The warm atmosphere is due in some part to the simplicity and generosity of the space – high walls of glowing Cotswold stone – and in large part to the craftspeople whose commitment helped to restore the building. The nesting holes for doves high up in the eaves were left intact by the stonemasons and then glazed so as to weatherproof the space. All the restoration has been done with a light hand, fulfilling my wish that the building should appear untouched and natural, retaining as far as possible its original appearance and intent.

It is always a challenge to make an agricultural space function as a domestic one and still preserve the qualities that made you fall in love with it in the first place. Working with traditional rural makers has helped retain its honesty. So, we used a willow worker for the banisters leading up to the mezzanine, a hurdle maker for the cupboard doors we found and rush weavers to make large rugs to soften the concrete floor.

I love collecting and like to have around me here things that I cherish and find inspirational. The painted cupboards by the entrance contain textiles found in Indian and French markets. By the fireplace I have a long line of pots. One favourite, pictured, is a Lucie Rie bowl. It is the most simple and quiet of pieces, a dish pared down to the essentials and resonating with the character of the maker. It seems to embody this building.

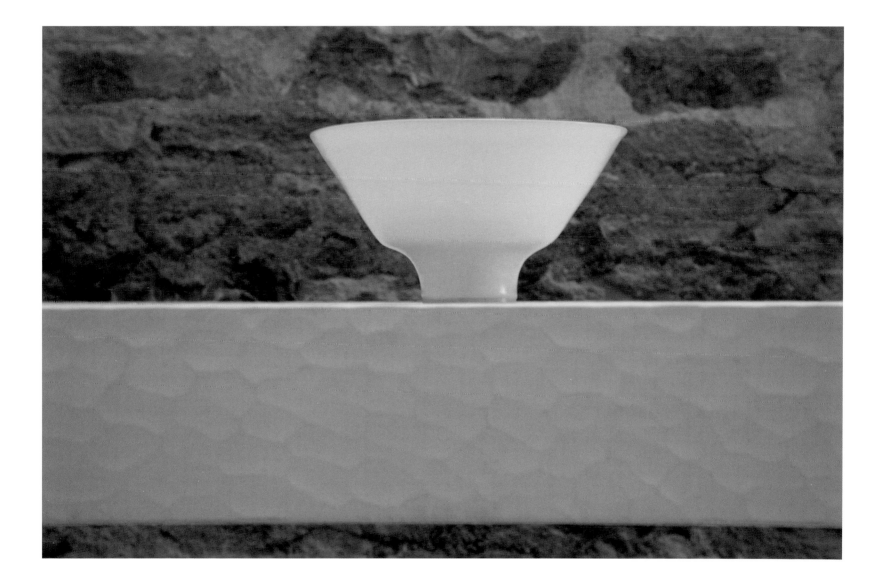

Benedict Cumberbatch

The library
The Garrick Club, London

I was still at school when I first visited the Garrick Club and my father took me to the library. In my memory it always featured as an enormous room, very grand and impressive. Visiting it now, years later, it appears quite small – which in fact it is. It still retains, though, a particular aura, which I sensed on my first visit.

As an actor accustomed to reading scripts consisting generally of photocopied pages roughly bound together, it is an incredible luxury to be able to read those same scripts in beautiful editions, frequently very early ones, printed on heavy paper and in generous type. There is a special thrill in handling a book that might have been held by Irving, Forbes-Robertson or Beerbohm Tree, a thrill that is hard to convey to anyone outside the acting profession.

This place is an oasis of quiet: a stone's throw from Charing Cross Road and the theatre district on one side, and from Covent Garden on the other. It is possible to sit here in silence, surrounded by volumes full of original playbills – Edmund Kean (referred to as 'Mr' Kean) in *Richard III* or *Othello*. It enables one to touch, as it were, the past of the magic world of theatre.

William Dalrymple

Zafar Mahal
Delhi

Not far from my farm on the southern edge of Delhi lie the ruins of the summer palace of the last Mughal emperors. It is named Zafar Mahal, the Palace of Victory, and sometimes, on winter afternoon walks, I wander over there to sit amid the broken doorways and shattered cusps of the Mughal arches, and ponder on the rise and fall of empires.

Zafar Mahal, built in the 1840s for Zafar, the last Mughal Emperor, is today an atmospheric but deeply melancholy spot. Somehow it still retains the quality of tragic ruination that marked the last days of Mughal Delhi, known as the Delhi Twilight, just before the British destroyed both the Mughal dynasty and the syncretic culture they created there. Yet, despite its crumbling beauty, the old summer palace receives little protection from the government and has now become the preferred gathering place of the ne'er-do-wells of Mehrauli: gamblers, drunks and heroin addicts haunt its gutted courtyards. Junkies sneak behind the pillars of the Durbar Hall with their silver foil and brown sugar and boxes of matches; in the former Elephant Stables the afternoon drinkers knock back shots of Bagpiper as they throw down their cards in disgust at their unlucky hands. Teenagers bat their cricket balls into the delicate Mughal lattices of the zenana quarters. Every few months another pillar is knocked over or another fragile *jali* is broken.

Zafar was a skilled calligrapher, a discriminating patron, an inspired creator of gardens and a mystical poet, and his palace frequently played host to poets and miniature painters. But now the cusped arches of the chambers where the Emperor once held his famous *mushairas* or poetic symposia are slowly collapsing, mute witnesses to the fall of the great Mughal dynasty; only pigeons declaim here today.

Following the Indian Mutiny, Zafar's sons were killed and he himself sent into exile, while the fragile court culture he had faithfully nourished underwent a rapid and complete decline. Today, more than 150 years later, Delhi feels as if it is fast moving away from its Mughal past. In the modern Indian capital an increasingly wealthy Punjabi middle class now live in an aspirational bubble of fast-rising shopping malls, espresso bars and multiplexes. This emerging middle-class India has its eyes firmly fixed on the future, with the consequence that Delhi's past is often tragically neglected.

Sometimes, sitting amid the ruins of Zafar Mahal, I wonder what Zafar would have made of all this. Looking out over the Sufi shrine that abuts his palace, I suspect he would somehow have made his peace with the fast-changing cyber-India of call centres and software parks that are now slowly overpowering the last remnants of his world. After all, realism and acceptance were always qualities Zafar excelled in. For all the tragedy of his life, Zafar was able to see that the world continued to turn, and that however much the dogs might bark, the great caravan of life moves on.

Trevor McDonald

The Committee Room
The Oval, London

The choice of location for this photograph is significant to me. I have always rated the Committee Room of the Surrey County Cricket Club as the finest place in the world to watch cricket. No place affords a better view of what's going on out in the middle! As if that was not a sufficiently good reason for having the picture taken at the club's famous ground, the Oval, I have been asked to be the club's president for the season beginning in the spring of 2013. I can think of no greater honour.

But there's more. In my years growing up in Trinidad I succumbed to cricket as a Caribbean obsession. How the West Indies cricket team – perhaps one of the few reminders that our tiny islands are in every sense a family of small nation-states – performed at home and abroad, especially against England, became the focus of our island lives and the unending subject of fierce national discourse.

I have followed the fortunes of England and the West Indies at almost every ground in Britain, in India, in Australia, and in South Africa. Being president of Surrey is the icing on the cake.

The Duchess of Northumberland

The tree house
Alnwick Castle, Northumberland

I wanted to build a tree house because I believe that everyone loves them. Why be at ground level when you can be 60 feet high in the trees? I didn't have a tree house as a child, but I have noticed that what applies to children almost always applies to the elderly.

One might wonder why I chose this as my favourite place rather than somewhere in Alnwick Castle itself. Of course the castle is incredibly grand and full of beautiful things, but it is somewhere that is essentially complete and can pretty well be left to look after itself. I built the tree house in this location because it was the only place that had a cluster of mature trees that could provide the perfect canopy for the building. The trees – lime trees – are over 70 feet tall. It was a difficult build because we had to be very careful not to damage these mature trees. We also have to carry out continuous health-and-safety checks to ensure that the branches are safe.

When I started this project, I had no precise idea what I wanted since I hadn't seen any similar building on this scale before. However, I knew that I most definitely did not want the end result to look like a new building. Rather, I wanted it to look as if it had evolved over a period of years; that it had been gradually added to – and with a variety and 'patchwork' of woods. I wanted it to feel 'magical'. To achieve this, every part of the building, inside and out, had to be carefully designed.

There is a team of staff working in the castle who know more about it than I will ever know. I need to be busy and I like to be busy. I'm interested in people, and the community programmes in the garden are what I most enjoy. They will keep me busy for the rest of my life. Although I have always been interested in gardening, what I'm more interested in is how gardening and gardens can enhance lives, even change lives.

A new experience – an unusual experience – is what enhances lives.

Otis Ferry

The stables
Seaton Delaval, Northumberland

Ever since I can remember, I have felt happier surrounded by nature than in the city. I prefer the company of animals to that of people; there are bonds of communication with animals that are not made with language but with a sort of sixth sense.

One of the many joys I find in foxhunting is its timeless quality. It is a sport untouched by modern technology that has remained virtually unchanged for over two hundred years.

Something that critics of foxhunting never understand is the feeling that a lover of hunting has for the fox. It may seem paradoxical, but he regards the fox with reverence, even admiration. There is a specific season for hunting, which respects the period needed for the fox to breed and rear its cubs. The fox is not considered vermin, like a rat, as a thing that should simply be destroyed.

Moreover, contrary to popular belief, the hunt is not primarily about killing the fox. For me, as a Master of Foxhounds, a day's hunting without catching the fox can be just as wonderful as any other, an idea that would be incomprehensible to an outsider – or to someone shooting, for whom the day is largely judged by how many birds have been shot and which seems to me a highly egotistical sport. In hunting, one can admire the huntsman and the hounds almost as an observer, and of course there is also the important bond between rider and horse.

Today, although horses may be much loved, one cannot imagine anyone lavishing the same care on their stables as on their own house, which is what happened at Seaton Delaval. The stables here are an outstanding example of attitudes to the horse at a time when horses and all things equine were of paramount importance in everyday life. Stables nowadays are rarely places of beauty – function and economy taking precedence over aesthetics – but in these stables at Seaton Delaval there is as much attention to detail as in a house of the period. Unlike stables built today, which are mostly of timber, in this tall stone building the air remains cool even in the height of summer: an important factor for the horses. The fire that devastated the main house in 1822, resulting in its effective abandonment, spared the stables, leaving them virtually intact. Unused since then, their atmosphere, as in a painting by Stubbs, is incredibly evocative.

Biographies

Carole Bamford

Carole Bamford is best known for establishing the Daylesford Organic Farmshops chain and the Bamford brand of natural clothing, body products and homewares, as well as being a director of JCB, the family firm. Her charitable and philanthropic activities include educational projects in India, South America and the USA in addition to extensive work with the NSPCC.

Stephen Bayley

Stephen Bayley is an author, critic, consultant, curator and lecturer. A co-creator of the V&A's influential Boilerhouse Project, which evolved into the Design Museum, he was also creative director of the exhibition at the Millennium Dome. The architecture and design correspondent of *The Observer* since 2007, he has written more than a dozen books on design, consumer culture and aesthetics.

The Duke of Beaufort

The 11th Duke of Beaufort, David Somerset, lives at his family's ancestral seat, Badminton House, which plays host to the famous Horse Trials. His career has included stints as hereditary keeper of Raglan Castle and president of the British Horse Society; he became a partner of Marlborough Fine Art in 1948 and has served as the gallery's chairman since 1964.

Cressida Bell

Cressida Bell is a designer specialising in textiles and interiors. Influenced by her Bloomsbury Group forebears (her grandmother was Vanessa Bell and her father Quentin Bell) but working in her own distinctive style, her output ranges from stationery to murals, carpets to furnishing fabrics. She is a graduate of the Royal College of Art.

Alan Bennett

Alan Bennett is a playwright, screenwriter, actor and author. Achieving initial success with the satirical revue *Beyond the Fringe* in the 1960s, his more recent work has included the *Talking Heads* television series and the stage plays *The History Boys* (winner of six Tony Awards), *The Habit of Art*, *Cocktail Sticks* and *People*.

Jasper Conran

Jasper Conran is a designer whose signature aesthetic – a blend of classic British elegance with a cheeky irreverence – has been applied to menswear, womenswear, accessories, fragrance, furniture and homewares. As well as producing his own collections, he has also collaborated with Wedgwood (china), Waterford (crystal) and the Designers Guild (fabrics and wallpapers).

Benedict Cumberbatch

Benedict Cumberbatch is a film, TV and stage actor best known for his starring roles in the BBC dramas *Sherlock* and *Parade's End*. His film roles have included William Pitt in *Amazing Grace* and Paul Marshall in *Atonement*; his portrayal of Bernard in *Small Island* earned him a BAFTA award for best supporting actor.

William Dalrymple

William Dalrymple is a writer, historian and curator with a particular interest in India and the Islamic world. His award-winning books include *Nine Lives: In Search of the Sacred in Modern India*, *The Last Mughal* and *White Mughals*. His latest publication is *Return of a King: The Battle for Afghanistan 1839–42*.

Monty Don

Monty Don is a gardening writer and broadcaster. Best known for presenting the BBC's *Gardeners' World*, he has also created a number of TV series including *Monty's Italian Gardens*, *Around the World in 80 Gardens*, *Fork to Fork* and *My Dream Farm*. He was *The Observer*'s gardening editor from 1994 to 2006.

James Dyson

James Dyson is an industrial designer and chief engineer at Dyson. Renowned as the inventor of the Dual Cyclone bagless vacuum cleaner, his recent inventions include the Dyson Ball, the ContraRotator and the Airblade. In 2002 he set up a foundation to support design and engineering education and in 2007 was awarded a knighthood.

Otis Ferry

Otis Ferry is joint master of the South Shropshire Hunt and a champion of country pursuits. He has been arrested and charged several times for his pro-hunting political activities and even on one occasion convicted; his most famous stunt involved breaking into the chamber of the House of Commons during a debate.

Stephen Fry

Stephen Fry is an actor, comedian, author, director, broadcaster and game show host. Since rising to fame in *A Bit of Fry and Laurie*, *Jeeves and Wooster* and *Blackadder*, he has starred in numerous plays, films and TV series, written four best-selling novels and presented several documentaries. He currently hosts the BBC quiz show *QI*.

Gilbert & George

Gilbert Proesch and George Passmore are a collaborative duo who met in 1967 as students at St Martins School of Art. They are known for their distinctive appearance (seeing themselves as 'living sculptures') and for their graphic-style photo-based artworks, many inspired by the East End of London where they have lived and worked for over 40 years.

Nelufar Hedayat

Nelufar Hedayat is a TV presenter and documentary maker who came to public attention in 2010 with the critically acclaimed *Women, Weddings, War and Me*. She has since made several further documentaries for the BBC and currently presents CBBC's *Newsround*. She arrived in England at the age of six from her war-torn homeland of Afghanistan.

P. D. James

P. D. James (Baroness James of Holland Park) is a crime writer most famous for her series of detective novels starring policeman and poet Adam Dalgliesh, many of which have been adapted for television. Her other writings include essays, short stories, two Cordelia Gray mysteries and her latest novel, *Death Comes to Pemberley*.

Simon Jenkins

Simon Jenkins is an author and journalist. He writes for *The Guardian* as well as broadcasting for the BBC. A former editor of *The Times* and *London's Evening Standard*, he is now chairman of the National Trust. He has written many books on politics, history and architecture, including *England's Thousand Best Churches* and *England's Thousand Best Houses*.

Felicity Kendal

Felicity Kendal was born into a theatrical family in India and first performed on stage at the age of three. Probably best known for playing Barbara Good in the TV series *The Good Life*, she has appeared in numerous stage and screen roles over a 45-year career, most recently being cast as Sheila in Alan Ayckbourn's *Relatively Speaking*.

Tim Knox

Tim Knox is an architectural historian. Following stints at the Royal Institute of British Architects and the National Trust, he was director of Sir John Soane's Museum, where he masterminded the restoration of the two houses flanking Soane's original museum. He has recently been appointed director of the Fitzwilliam Museum in Cambridge.

Willie Landels

Willie Landels is an Italian-born artist and designer whose best-known creation is undoubtedly the Throw-Away armchair, first conceived in 1963 and still manufactured by Zanotta today. Art editor of *Queen* magazine from 1965, in 1970 he founded *Harpers & Queen*, acting as its editor and art director for 15 years.

Trevor McDonald

Trevor McDonald is a newsreader, journalist and biographer who had a long career with ITN, reading the *News at Ten* and presenting the current affairs programme *Tonight with Trevor McDonald*. Born in Trinidad, he is notable for having been the first black newsreader in the UK; he was knighted for services to journalism in 1999.

David Mlinaric

David Mlinaric is an interior designer whose clients have ranged from Lord Rothschild and Mick Jagger to the National Trust, the Royal Opera House and the V&A. He has decorated interiors all over the world, from the National Gallery in London to the British embassies in Washington and Paris via houses in Ireland, Italy, Corfu, and Mustique.